J. W Randolph

Everlasting Joy

Adapted to the Use of Public and Private Worship

J. W Randolph

Everlasting Joy
Adapted to the Use of Public and Private Worship

ISBN/EAN: 9783337290191

Printed in Europe, USA, Canada, Australia, Japan

Cover: Foto ©Thomas Meinert / pixelio.de

More available books at **www.hansebooks.com**

THE
Everlasting Joy.

ADAPTED TO THE USE OF

Public and Private Worship, Sabbath Schools,
Prayer Meetings; also, Anniversary
Occasions, etc., etc.,

BY

J. W. RANDOLPH.

PUBLISHED BY
THOS. GOGGAN & BRO.,
Galveston, Texas.

PREFATORY.

In the arrangement of this book it will be seen that the Author has not confined himself to any particular method. The music is new, while the sentiments expressed in verses are well adapted to the purpose and intention of this work. For the Church, the Home and Sabbath School, as well as for Prayer Meetings, the work will prove eminently fitted. Each tune has its own inspiring influence and was composed according to the dictation of its poetic thought. To cheer the heart and elevate the soul of man and to glorify God with songs of joy is its mission.

J. W. RANDOLPH.

Copyrighted, 1884, *by THOS. GOGGAN & BRO.,*
Galveston, Texas,

EVERLASTING JOY.

THE HOUSE OF PRAYER.

A CROWN OF LIFE.

Animated.

J. W. R.

1. O when shall I see Jesus, And reign with Him above, And from the flowing fountain Drink everlasting love. When shall I be delivered From this vain world of sin, And with my blessed Jesus Drink endless pleasures in.
2. But now I am a soldier, My Captain's gone before, He's given me my orders, And tells me not to fear. And if I hold out faithful, A crown of life He'll give, And all His valiant soldiers Eternal life shall have.
3. Through grace I am determined to conquer though I die; And then away to Jesus On wings of love I'll fly. Farewell to sin and sorrow, I bid them both adieu: And you, my friends, prove faithful, And on your way pursue.
4. And if you meet with troubles and trials on the way, Then cast your care on Jesus, And don't forget to pray. Gird on the heavenly armor Of faith, and hope, and love, And when your warfare's ended, You'll reign with Him above
5. O! do not be discouraged, For Jesus is your friend, And if you long for knowledge, On Him you may depend; Neither will he upbraid you, Though often you request; He'll give you grace to conquer, And take you home to rest.

Chorus.

A crown, A crown, A crown of life He gives to all, A crown of life He gives to all, Yes, all His valient soldier's Eternal life shall have.

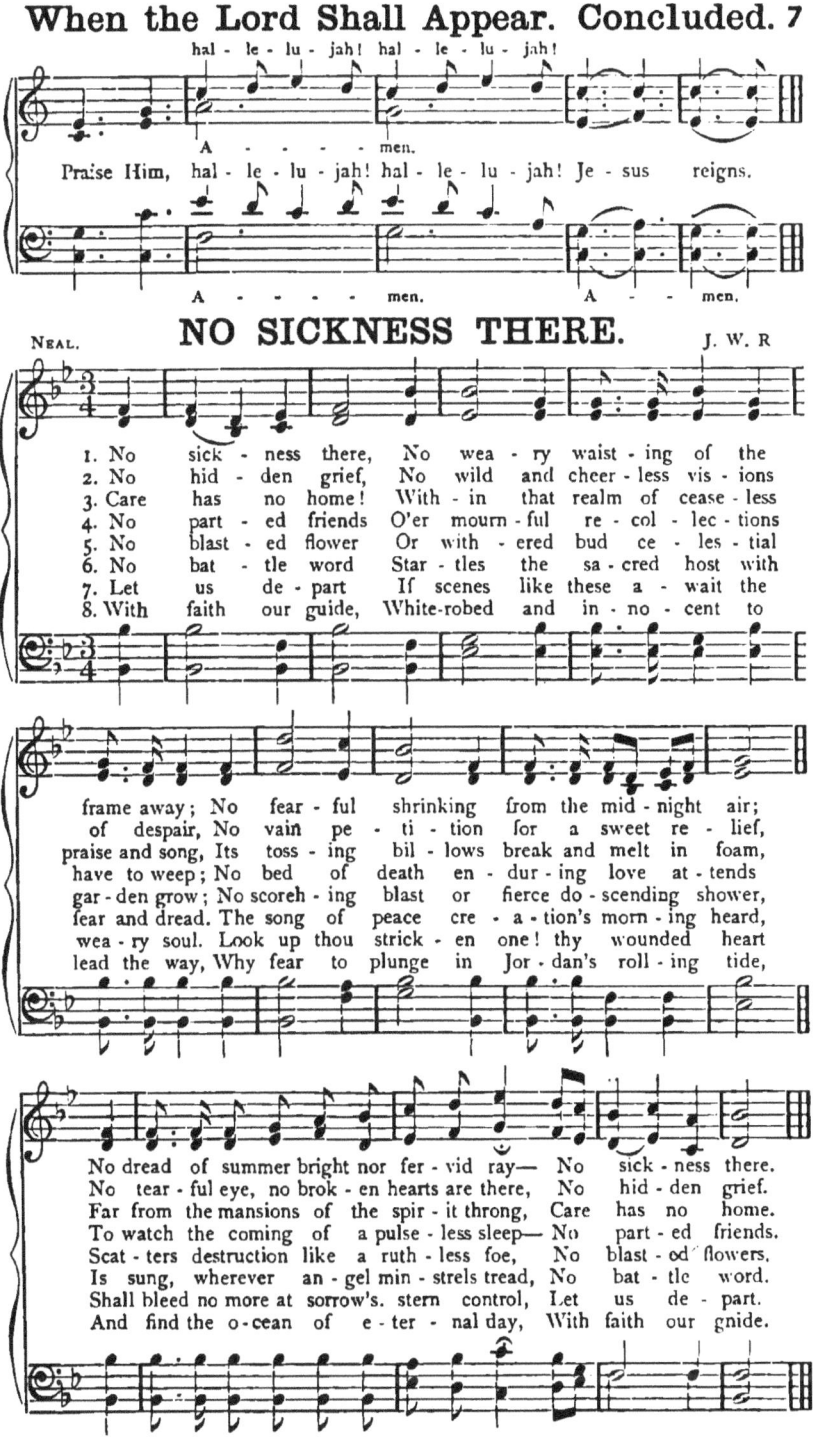

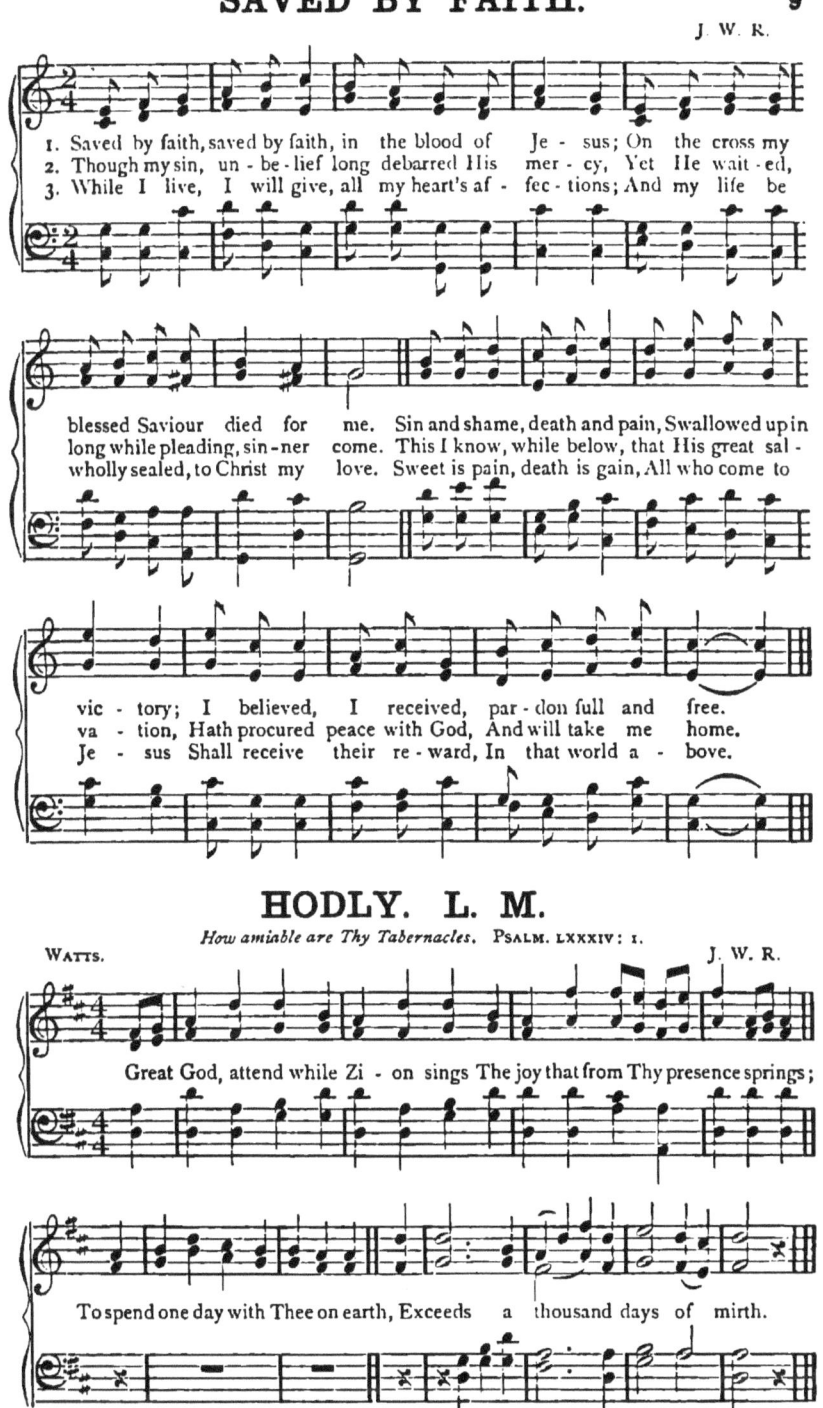

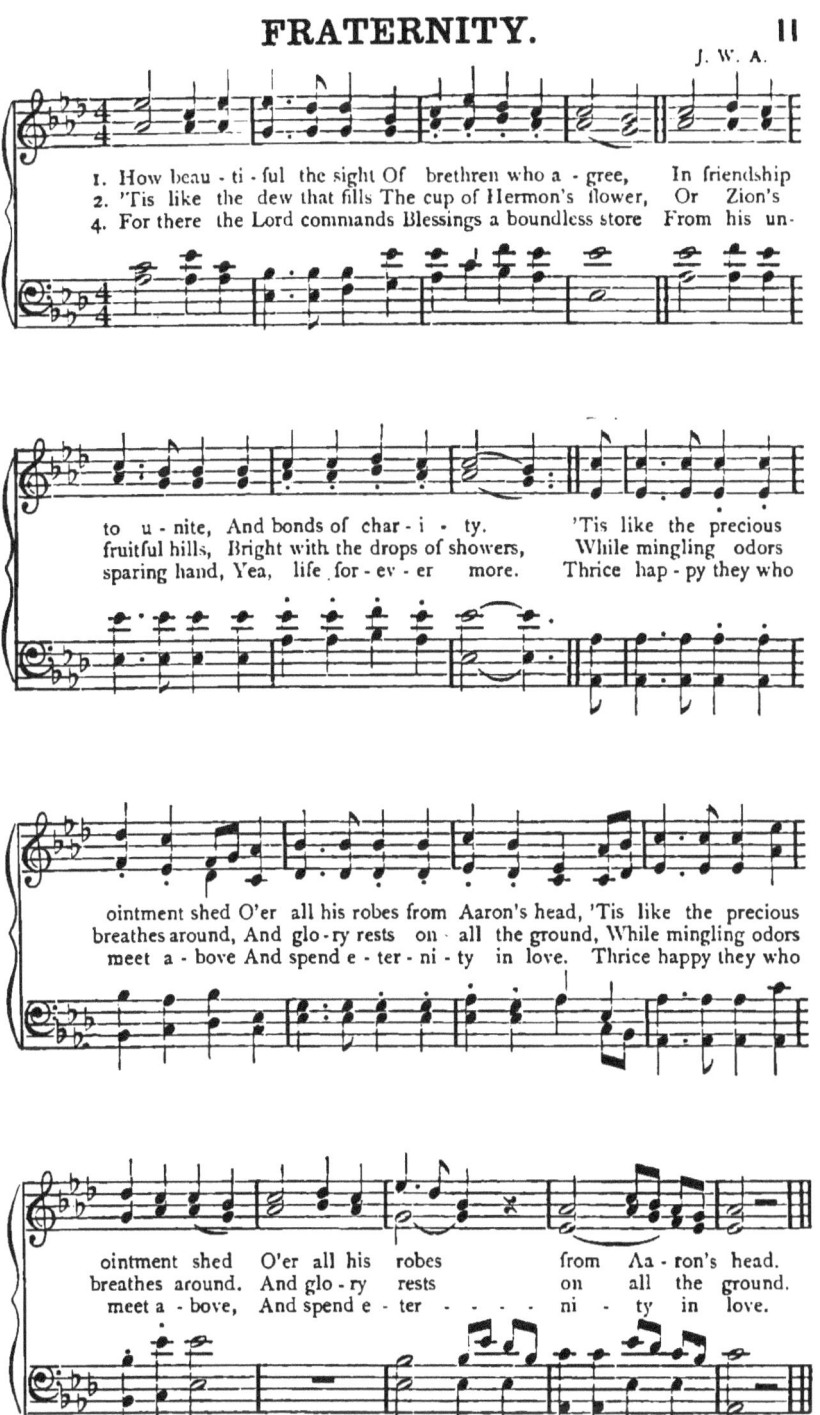

PARTING-HYMN.

J. W. R.

1. Peaceful-ly, tender-ly, Here as we part, The farewell that lingers Be
2. Thoughtfully, careful-ly, Solemn and slow! Tears are be-dewing The

D. S. Peacefully, tenderly, Here as we part The farewell that lingers Be

breathed from the heart; { No place more fit-ting, O house of the Lord,
{ Here be it spok-en, That last prayerful word,
path that we go; { Per-ils be-fore us We know not to-day—
{ Kindly and safe-ly, O Lord, lead the way.

breathed from the heart.

3. Upwardly, steadfastly,
   Gaze on that brow:
   Jesus, our Leader,
   Reigns conqueror now.
   His steps let us follow,
   His sufferings dare,
   Go up to glory,
   His blessedness share.

4. Patiently, cheerfully,
   Up, and depart
   To labor and duty
   With gladness of heart;
   The ransomed, with triumph,
   To Zion we'll bring,
   Shouting salvation
   To Jesus, our King,

DOVER. S. M.

ENGLISH.

Great is the Lord our God, And let his praise be great;

He makes the churches his abode, His most delight-ful seat.

EASTER-HYMN. Concluded.

3. Now, ye saints, lift up your eyes!
   Hallelujah, Hallelujah!
   Now to glory see him rise,
   Hallelujah!
   In long triumph, up the sky—
   Hallelujah, Hallelujah!
   Up to waiting worlds on high,
   Hallelujah!

4. Heav'n displays her portal wide!
   Glorious hero, through them ride!
   King of Glory! mount the throne—
   Thy great Father's and Thy own.

5. Praise Him, all ye heavenly choirs!
   Hallelujah, Hallelujah;
   Praise, and sweep your golden lyres!
   Hallelujah!
   Shout, O earth, in rapt'rous song,
   Hallelujah, Hallelujah!
   Let the strains be sweet and strong,
   Hallelujah!

6. Ev'ry note with wonder swell,
   Sin o'erthrown, and captiv'd hell!
   Where is hell's once dreaded king?
   Where, O death, thy mortal sting?

TRIBUTE. L. M.

WATTS.   J. W. R.

1. Be-fore Je-ho-vah's aw-ful throne, Ye nations bow with sa-cred joy; Know that the Lord is God alone, The Lord is God alone, He can create and He destroy,
2. His sovereign power, without our aid, Made us of clay and form'd us men, And when like wand'ring sheep we stray'd, Like wand'ring sheep we stray'd, He brought us to His fold again.
3. We are His people—we His care— Our souls, and all our mortal frame: What lasting honors shall we rear, Lasting honors shall we rear, Almighty Maker, to Thy name!

4. We'll crowd Thy gates with thankful songs,
   High as the heavens our voices raise;
   And earth, with her ten thousand tongues,
   Shall fill Thy courts with sounding praise!

5. Wide as the world is Thy command!
   Vast as eternity Thy love!
   Firm as a rock Thy truth shall stand,
   When rolling years shall cease to move!

FREEDOM'S JUBILEE.

W. H. YOUNG.
PROF. A. J. MOORE.

1. Sons of freedom, wake to glory, Let your anthems fill the sky! Children, men and fathers hoa-ry, Raise your voi-ces loud and high; Join your voi-ces all to-geth-er! Sing the song of lib-er-ty, Freedom reigns on land and wa-ter, This is freedom's ju-bi-lee!

2. Sons of freedom, join the chorus, Sing together with ac-cord; Brighter days are now before us, Let us sing and praise the Lord; Praise the Lord who reigns in heaven, On the earth and on the sea! Ev-'ry shack-el he has riv-en, He has let th' oppressed go free.

3. Sons of freedom, wake to glory, Tune your hearts in grateful lays! Freedom reigns, O blessed sto-ry, Sing a joy-ful song of praise! Praise the Lord with heart and voi-ces, He has gained the vic-to-ry! Ev-'ry freed-man now re-joi-ces, On the land and on the sea!

Freedom reigns on land and water, This is freedom's ju-bi-lee, etc.
Ev-'ry freedman now re-joi-ces, etc.
Ev-'ry shack-el he has riv-en, etc.

Chorus. Vivace.

Sons of freedom, wake to glory! Let your anthems fill the sky! Children,

FREEDOM'S JUBILEE. Concluded. 17

men and fathers hoary, Raise your voi - ces loud and high!

WINDHAM. L. M.

READ.

Mournful.

Broad is the road that leads to death, And thousands walk to - gether there;

But wisdom shows a narrow path, With here and there a trav - el - ler.

One thing needful. L. M.

1. WHY will ye waste on trifling cares
That life which God's compassion spares;
While, in the various range of thought,
The one thing needful is forgot?

2. Shall God invite you from above?
Shall Jesus urge his dying love?
Shall troubled conscience give you pain?
And all these pleas unite in vain?

3. Not so your eyes will always view
Those objects which you now pursue:
Not so will heaven and hell appear
When death's decisive hour is near.

4. Almighty God! Thy power impart;
Fix deep conviction on each heart;
Nor let us waste on trifling cares
That life which thy compassion spares.

EXALTATION. L. M.

MONTGOMERY. J. M. R.

Maestoso.

1. Who are these in bright array, Shining like the noonday sun, In the midst of perfect day, Nearest the e-ter-nal throne?
2. Round the al-tar saints confess, If their robes are white as snow, 'Twas the Saviour's wondrous grace, And His blood that made them so.
3. Who were these? on earth they dwelt; Sinners once, of Adam's race; Guilt, and fear, and suffering felt; But were saved by sovereign grace.
4. They were mortal, too, like us: Ah! when we, like them, must die, May our souls, translated thus, Triumph, reign and shine on high!

These are they that bore the cross,
Sufferers in His righteous cause,
Nobly for their Master stood;
Followers of the dying God!

MONTGOMERY. *Rev.* 7: 13-17.

1.
PALMS of glory, raiment bright,
  Crowns that never fade away,
Gird and deck the saints of light;
  Priest, and kings, and conquerors they.

2.
Yet the conquerors bring their palms
  To the Lamb amidst the throne,
And proclaim in joyful psalms
  Victory through His cross alone,

3.
Kings for harps their crowns resign,
  Crying, as they strike the chord,
"Take the kingdom, it is Thine,
  King of kings, and Lord of lords!"

20. OLD HUNDRED. L. M.

Watts. — *Luther.*

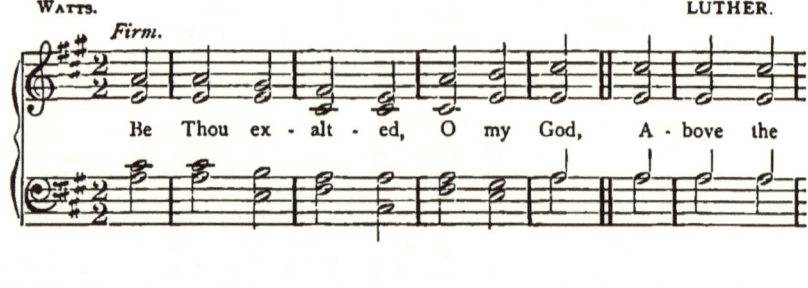
Be Thou ex-alt-ed, O my God, A-bove the

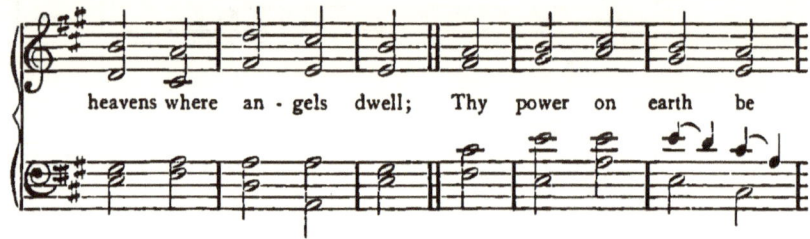
heavens where an-gels dwell; Thy power on earth be

known a-broad, And land to land Thy won-ders tell.

S. M.

TUNE ABSENCE.
Absent in the flesh—present in the spirit.

1. AND let our bodies part,
   To different climes repair;
   Still and forever joined in heart
   The friends of Jesus are.

2. O let us still proceed
   In Jesus' work below;
   And following our triumphant Head
   To further conquests go.

3. O let our heart and mind,
   Great God, to Thee ascend,
   That haven of repose to find,
   Where all our labors end;

4. Where all our toils are o'er,
   Our suffering and our pain:
   Who meet on that eternal shore
   Shall never part again.—WESLEY.

C. M.

TUNE WRIGHT.
Homage and devotion.

1. WITH sacred joy we lift our eyes
   To those bright realms above,
   That glorious temple in the skies,
   Where dwells eternal Love.

2. Before the gracious throne we bow
   Of heaven's almighty King;
   Here we present the solemn vow,
   And hymns of praise we sing.

3. O Lord, while in Thy house we kneel,
   With trust and holy fear,
   Thy mercy and Thy truth reveal
   And lend a gracious ear.

4. With fervor teach our hearts to pray,
   And tune our lips to sing;
   Nor from Thy presence cast away
   The sacrifice we bring.

As Down in the Sunless Retreat of the Ocean.

2. As still to the star of its worship, though clouded,
The needle points faithfully o'er the dim sea;
So, dark as I roam through this wintry world shrouded,
The hope of my spirit turns trembling to Thee,
My God, trembling to Thee, True, fond, trembling to Thee!

PARK STREET. L. M.
VENUA.

Hark! how the cho-ral song of heaven Swells full of peace and joy a-bove; Hark! how they strike their gold-en harps, And raise the tune-ful notes of love, And raise the tune-ful notes of love.

TUNE LULU.   Harvest-Home.   **7s, double.**

1. COME, ye thankful people, come,
    Raise the song of Harvest home!
   All is safely gathered in,
   Ere the winter-storms begin;
   God, our Maker, doth provide
   For our wants to be supplied;
   Come to God's own temple, come,
   Raise the song of Harvest-home!

2. We ourselves are God's own field,
   Fruit unto his praise to yield;
   Wheat and tares together sown,
   Unto joy our sorrow grown;
   First the blade, and then the ear,
   Then the full corn shall appear:
   Lord of harvest, grant that we
   Wholesome grain and pure may be!

3. For the Lord our God shall come,
   And shall take His harvest home!
   From His field shall purge away
   All that doth offend, that day;
   Give His angels charge at last
   In the fires the tares to cast,
   But the fruitful ears to store
   In His garner evermore.

4. Then, thou Church triumphant, come,
   Raise the song of Harvest-home!
   All are safely gathered in,
   Free from sorrow, free from sin;
   There forever, purified,
   In God's garner to abide;
   Come, ten thousand angels, come,
   Raise the glorious Harvest-home!

The Church in the wilderness.

1. FAR down the ages now,
   Much of her journey done,
  The pilgrim church pursues her way,
   Until her crown be won.

2. The story of the past
   Comes up before her view:
  How well it seems to suit her still—
   Old, and yet ever new!

3. It is the oft-told tale
   Of sin and weariness—
  Of grace and love yet flowing down
   To pardon and to bless.

4. No wider is the gate,
   No broader is the way,
  No smoother is the ancient path,
   That leads to life and day.

AH, GUILTY SINNER! 27

J. W. R.

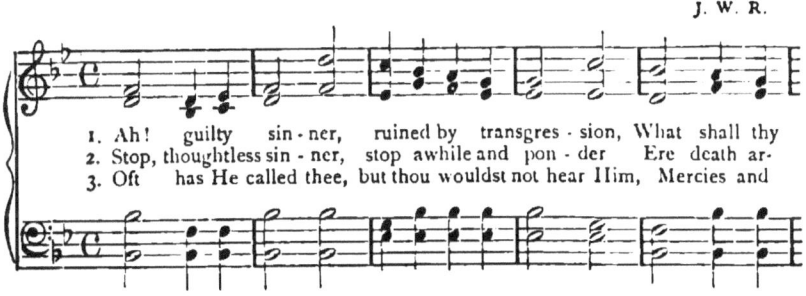

1. Ah! guilty sin-ner, ruined by transgres-sion, What shall thy
2. Stop, thoughtless sin-ner, stop awhile and pon-der Ere death ar-
3. Oft has He called thee, but thou wouldst not hear Him, Mercies and

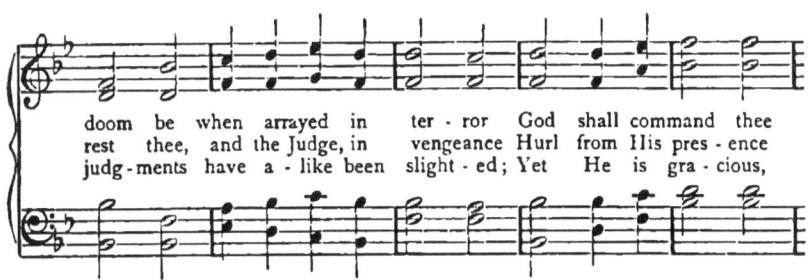

doom be when arrayed in ter-ror God shall command thee
rest thee, and the Judge, in vengeance Hurl from His pres-ence
judg-ments have a-like been slight-ed; Yet He is gra-cious,

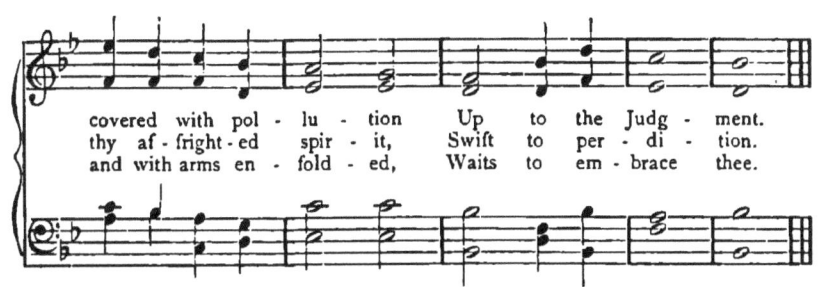

covered with pol-lu-tion Up to the Judg-ment.
thy af-fright-ed spir-it, Swift to per-di-tion.
and with arms en-fold-ed, Waits to em-brace thee.

4. Come, then, poor sinner, come away this moment,
   Just as you are, come, filthy and polluted,
   Come to the fountain open for the guilty;
       Jesus invites you.

5. But if you trifle with His gracious message,
   Cleave to the world and love its guilty pleasures,
   Mercy, grown weary, shall, in righteous judgment,
       Leave you for ever.

6. O! guilty sinner, hear the voice of warning;
   Fly to the Saviour, and embrace his pardon;
   So shall your spirit meet with joy triumphant,
       Death and the judgment.

MANTEO. Concluded.

in our spir-it speak; For we will hear Thy voice to-day, Nor turn our hard-ened hearts a-way.

2.
Speak in Thy gentlest tones of love,
Till all our best affections move;
We long to hear Thy gentle call,
And feel that Thou art all in all.

3.
To conscience speak Thy quickening word,
Till all its sense of sin is stirred;
For we would leave no stain of guile,
To cloud the radiance of Thy smile.

4.
Speak, Father, to the anxious heart,
Till every fear and doubt depart;
For we can find no home or rest,
Till with Thy Spirit's whispers blest.

5.
Speak to convince, forgive, console:
Childlike we yield to Thy control;
These hearts, too often closed before,
Would grieve Thy patient love no more.

C. WESLEY.

BALMOREL. S. M.

J. W. R

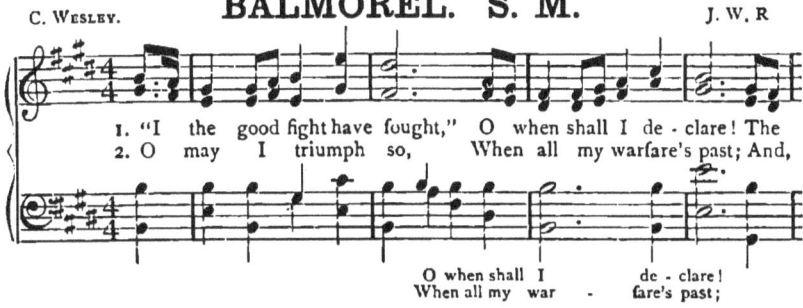

1. "I the good fight have fought," O when shall I de-clare! The vict'ry by my Saviour got I long with Paul to share, I long with Paul to share.
2. O may I triumph so, When all my warfare's past; And, dying, find my latest foe Under my feet at last, Under my feet at last!

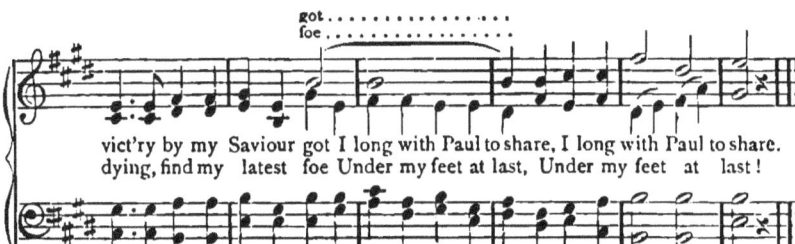

3. This blessed word be mine,
   Just as the port is gained,
   "Kept by the power of grace Divine,
   I have kept the faith maintained."

4. Th' apostles of my Lord,
   To whom it first was given,—
   They could not speak a greater word,
   Nor all the saints in heaven.

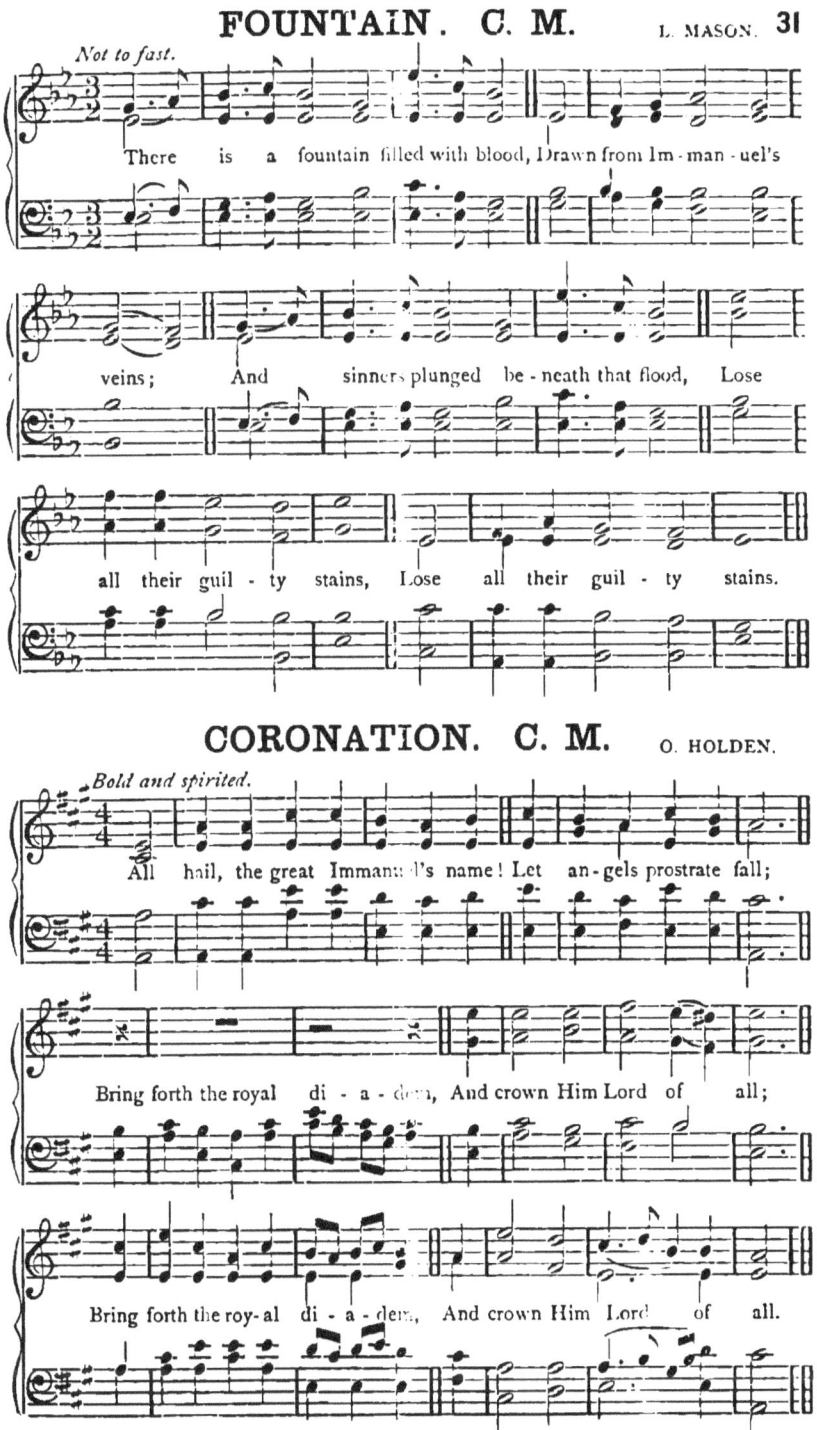

32. SINNER GO, WILL YOU GO?

F. LEDBETTER.

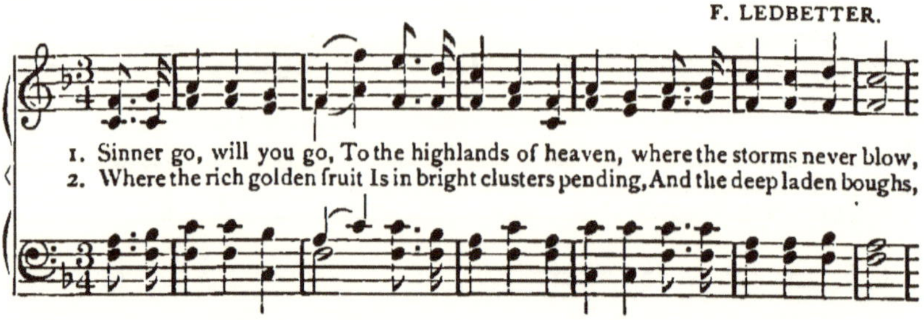

1. Sinner go, will you go, To the highlands of heaven, where the storms never blow,
And the long summer's given, Where the bright blooming flowers Their odors e-mitting, And the leaves of the bowers, Through the breezes are flit-ting?

2. Where the rich golden fruit Is in bright clusters pending, And the deep laden boughs,
Of life's fair tree are bending; And where life's crystal stream Is un-ceas-ing-ly flowing, And the verdure is green, And e-ter-nal-ly growing.

3. He's prepared thee a home—
Sinner canst thou believe it?
And invites thee to come,
Sinner, wilt thou receive it?
Where the saints robed in white
Cleansed in life's flowing fountain—
Shining beauteous and bright,
They inhabit the mountain;

4. O come, sinner, come,
For the tide is receding,
And the Saviour will soon,
And for ever, cease pleading,
Where no sin, nor dismay,
Neither trouble nor sorrow,
Will be felt for a day,
Nor be feared for the morrow.

CASTINGTON. L. M.

C. WESLEY.   STEPHEN CAMP.

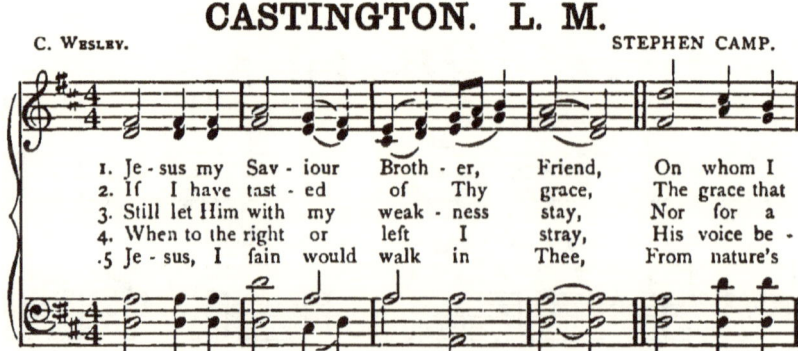

1. Je-sus my Sav-iour Broth-er, Friend, On whom I
2. If I have tast-ed of Thy grace, The grace that
3. Still let Him with my weak-ness stay, Nor for a
4. When to the right or left I stray, His voice be-
5. Je-sus, I fain would walk in Thee, From nature's

CASTINGTON. Concluded.

cast my ev - 'ry care,— On whom for all things I de - pend— Inspire, and then ac - cept my prayer.
sure sal - va - tion brings, If with me now Thy Spir - it stays, And hov'ring, hides me in His wings:
mo - ment's space de - part; E - vil and dan - ger turn a - way, And keep till He re - news my heart.
hind me may I hear, "Re - turn, and walk in Christ, thy way; Fly back to Christ, for sin is near!"
ev - 'ry path re - treat: Thou art my way; my lead - er be, And set up - on the rock my feet.

CYRUS. S. M.

C. WESLEY.   STEPHEN CAMP.

1. A charge to keep I have, A God to glo - ri - fy, A never dying soul to save, And fit it for the sky, And fit it for the sky.
2. To serve the present age, My calling to ful - fill, O may it all my powers engage, To do my Master's will, To do my Master's will.
3. Arm me with jealous care, As in Thy sight to live; And O, Thy ser - vant, Lord, prepare A strict account to give, A strict account to give.
4. Help me to watch and pray, And on Thyself re - ly; Assured if I my trust be - tray, I shall for - ev - er die, I shall forever die.

And fit it for the sky.
To do my Mas - ter's will.
A strict account to give.
I shall for - ev - er die.

"Must Simon Bear the Cross Alone?" 35

G. N. ALLEN. *Energetic.* J. W. R.

1. Must Simon bear the cross alone, And all the world go free?
   No, there's a cross for ev-ery one, And there's a cross for me.
   Yes, there's a cross on Cal-va-ry, Through which by faith the crown I see; To me 'tis pardon bringing, O that's the cross for me, O that's the cross for me!

2. How happy are the saints a-bove, Who once went mourning here!
   But now they taste un-ming-led love, And joy without a tear.
   For perfect love will dry the tear, And cast out all tormenting fear, Which round my heart is clinging; O that's the love for me, O that's the love for me!

3. We'll bear the consecrated cross,
   Till from the cross we're free;
   And then go home to wear the crown,
   For there's a crown for me.
   Yes, there's a crown in heaven above,
   The purchase of my Saviour's love,
   For me at His appearing;
   O that's the crown for me!

4. The saints shall hear the midnight cry;
   The Lord will then appear,
   And virgins rise with burning lamps,
   To meet him in the air;
   For there's a home in heaven prepared,
   A house by saints and angels shared,
   Where Christ is interceding;
   O that's the home for me!

DENHAM. TUNE DELAY NOT.—*Home.* 11s.

1. 'MID scenes of confusion and creature complaints,
   How sweet to my soul is communion with saints;
   To find at the banquet of mercy there's room,
   And feel in the presence of Jesus at home.

2. Sweet bonds, that unite all the children of peace;
   And thrice blesséd Jesus, whose love cannot cease;
   Though oft from Thy presence in sadness I roam,
   I long to behold Thee in glory at home.

3. While here in the valley of conflict I stray,
   O give me submission and strength as my day;
   In all my afflictions to Thee would I come,
   Rejoicing in hope of my glorious home.

4. I long, dearest Lord, in Thy beauty to shine;
   No more as an exile in sorrow to pine;
   And in Thy dear image arise from the tomb,
   With glorified millions to praise Thee at home.

DELAY NOT.

T. Hastings.
Slow.

1. De-lay not, de-lay not, O sin-ner, draw near, The waters of life are now flowing for thee; No price is demanded, the Saviour is here, Re-demption is purchased—sal-va-tion is free.
2. De-lay not, de-lay not! why long-er a-buse The love and compassion of Jesus our Lord! A fountain is opened; how canst thou refuse To wash and be cleansed in his par-doning blood?
3. De-lay not, de-lay not! O sin-ner, to come; For mercy still lin-gers, and calls thee to-day; Her voice is not heard in the vale of the tomb; Her mes-sage, unheeded, will soon pass a-way.

4. Delay not, delay not! the Spirit of grace,
   Long grieved and resisted, entreats thee to come;
   Beware, lest in darkness thou finish thy race,
   And sink to the vale of eternity's gloom.

5. Delay not, delay not! the hour is at hand,
   The earth shall dissolve and the heavens shall fade;
   The dead, small and great, in the judgment shall stand;
   What power, then, O sinner, shall lend thee its aid?

SEASONS. C. M.

PLEYEL.

Firm.

The flow-ery spring, at God's com-mand, Perfumes the

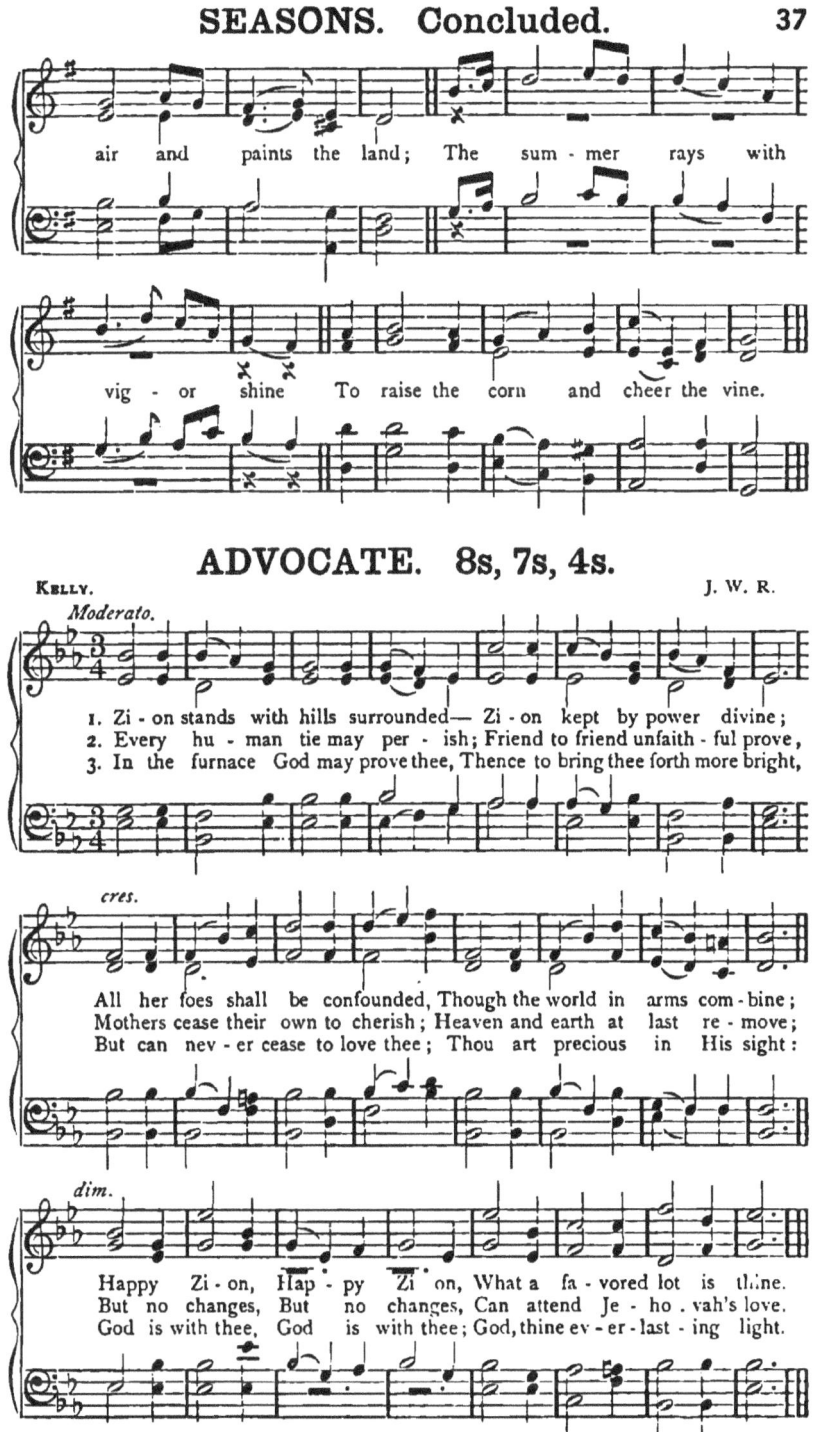

THE NATIVITY. Concluded.

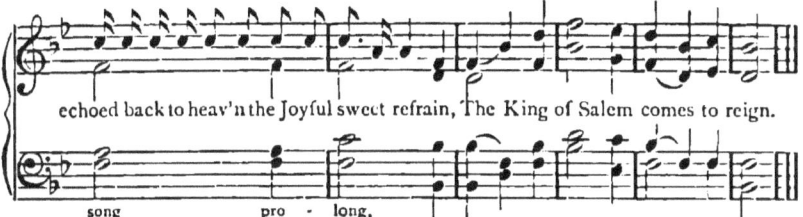

echoed back to heav'n the Joyful sweet refrain, The King of Salem comes to reign.

song   pro - long,

3.
Then swift to every startled eye
New streams of glory light the sky;
Heaven bursts her azure gates to pour
Her spirits on the midnight hour.

4.
On wheels of light, on wings of fame,
The glorious hosts of Zion came;
High heaven with songs of triumph rang,
While thus they struck their harps and sang.

5.
See, Mercy from her golden urn,
Pours a rich stream from them that mourn:
Behold! she binds with tender care
bleeding bosom of despair.

6.
He comes, to cheer the trembling heart,
Bids Satan and his hosts depart:
Again the day-star gilds the gloom,
Again the bowers of Eden bloom.

7.
O Zion, lift thy raptur'd eye,
The long-expected hour is nigh,
The joys of nature rise again,
The Prince of Salem comes to reign.

WILBERFORCE. S. M.

J. W. R.

1. Father, I stretch my hands to Thee. No other help I know;
2. What did Thine only Son en - dure, Before I drew my breath!

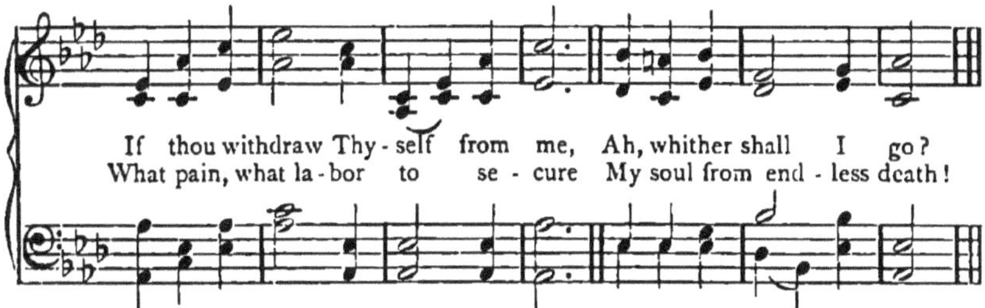

If thou withdraw Thy-self from me, Ah, whither shall I go?
What pain, what la-bor to se - cure My soul from end - less death!

3. O Jesus, could I this believe,
   I now should feel Thy pow'r;
   Now my poor soul Thou wouldst retrieve
   Nor let me wait one hour.

4. Author of faith, to Thee I lift
   My weary, longing eyes;
   O let me now receive that gift;
   My soul without it dies.

5. Surely Thou canst not let me die;
   O speak, and I shall live!
   And here I will unwearied lie
   Till Thou Thy Spirit give.

6. The worst of sinners would rejoice,
   Could they but see Thy face:
   O let me hear Thy quick'ning voice,
   And taste Thy pard'ning grace!

Behold Thy King, O Zion! Concluded.

ALL IS WELL.

J. W. R.   J. W. R.

1. O the val-ue of that word, All is well, all is well. Happy they who this have heard, All is well, all is well, 'Tis the soul in-spir-ing hope, Sweet'ning ev-'ry bit-ter cup, Lifting fainting spirits up, All is well, all is well.

1. This the only prop of all, all is well.
   That can never, never fall, all is well.
   'Tis the anchor of the soul, when the billows near it roll
   Bearing safely o'er the goal, all is well.

2. 'Tis religion's precious balm, all is well.
   Makes the raging winds a calm, all is well.
   Thus my pleasure midst the pain, either life or death is gain,
   Sing my soul thy sweet refrain, all is well.

4. When life's voyage I have made, all is well.
   When my barque aside is laid, all is well.
   When the trumpet's gladsome sound, calls the nations 'neath the ground,
   Let us all receive a crown, all is well.

MARK THE SOFT FALLING SNOW.

DODDRIDGE.   J. W. R.
Moderlato.

1. Mark the soft-falling snow, And the diffusive rain: To heaven, from whence it
2. Arrayed in beauteous green The hills and valleys shine, And man and beast are

Mark the Soft Falling Snow. Concluded. 43

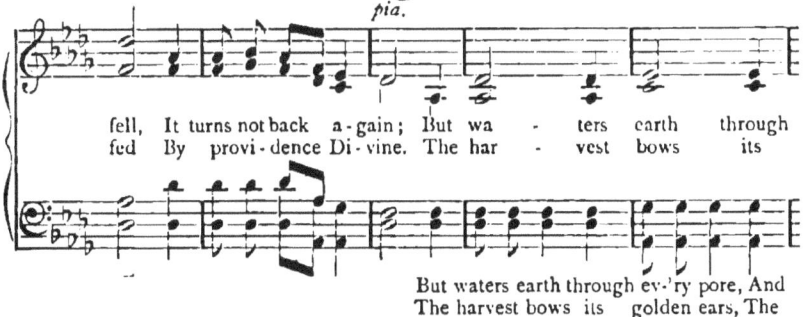

3.
So, saith the God of grace,
My gospel shall descend,
Almighty to effect
The purpose I intend.
Millions of souls shall feel its power,
And bear it down to millions more.

4.
Joy shall begin your march,
And peace protect your ways,
While all the mountains round
Echo melodious praise;
The vocal grove shall sing the God,
And every tree consenting nod.

NO NIGHT IN HEAVEN.

J. W. R.

44 NO NIGHT IN HEAVEN. Concluded.

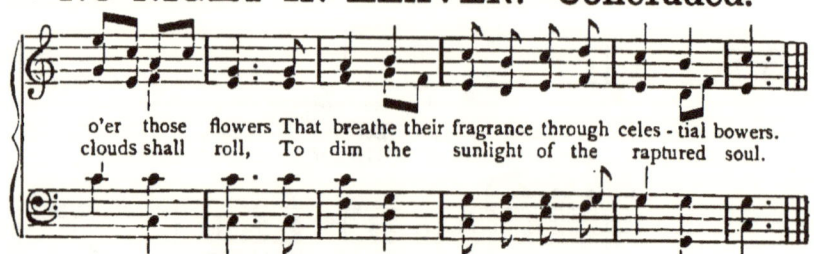

o'er those flowers That breathe their fragrance through celes-tial bowers.
clouds shall roll, To dim the sunlight of the raptured soul.

3. No night shall be in heaven. Forbid to sleep,
These eyes no more their mournful vigils keep;
Their fountains dried—their tears all wiped away—
They gaze undazzled on eternal day.

4. No night shall be in heaven—no sorrows reign;
No secret anguish, no corporeal pain;
No shivering limbs, no burning fever there;
No soul's eclipse, no winter of despair.

5. No night shall be in heaven, but endless noon—
No fast declining sun, no waning moon;
But there the Lamb shall yield perpetual light,
'Mid pastures green, and waters ever bright.

MY GOD I AM THINE.

C. Wesley. J. W. R.

1. My God, I am Thine, what a comfort di-vine, What a blessing to
2. True pleasures abound In the rap-turous sound; Who-ev-er hath
3. Yet onward I haste To the heav-en-ly feast: That, that is the

know that the Saviour is mine! In the hea-ven-ly Lamb thrice
found it, hath par-a-dise found: My Je-sus to know, And
full-ness; but this is the taste! And this I shall prove, Till

hap-py I am, My heart doth rejoice in the sound of His name.
feel His blood flow,—'Tis life ev-er-last-ing, 'tis heaven be-low.
with joy I remove To the heaven of heavens in Je-sus's love.

2. Now may the King descend,
   And fill His throne of grace;
   Thy sceptre, Lord, extend,
   While saints address Thy face:
   Let sinners feel Thy quick'ning word,
   And learn to know and fear the Lord.

3. Descend, celestial Dove,
   With all Thy quick'ning powers;
   Disclose a Saviour's love,
   And bless the sacred hours:
   Then shall my soul new life obtain,
   Nor Sabbath be indulged in vain.

CHAMP. C. P. M.

J. W. R.

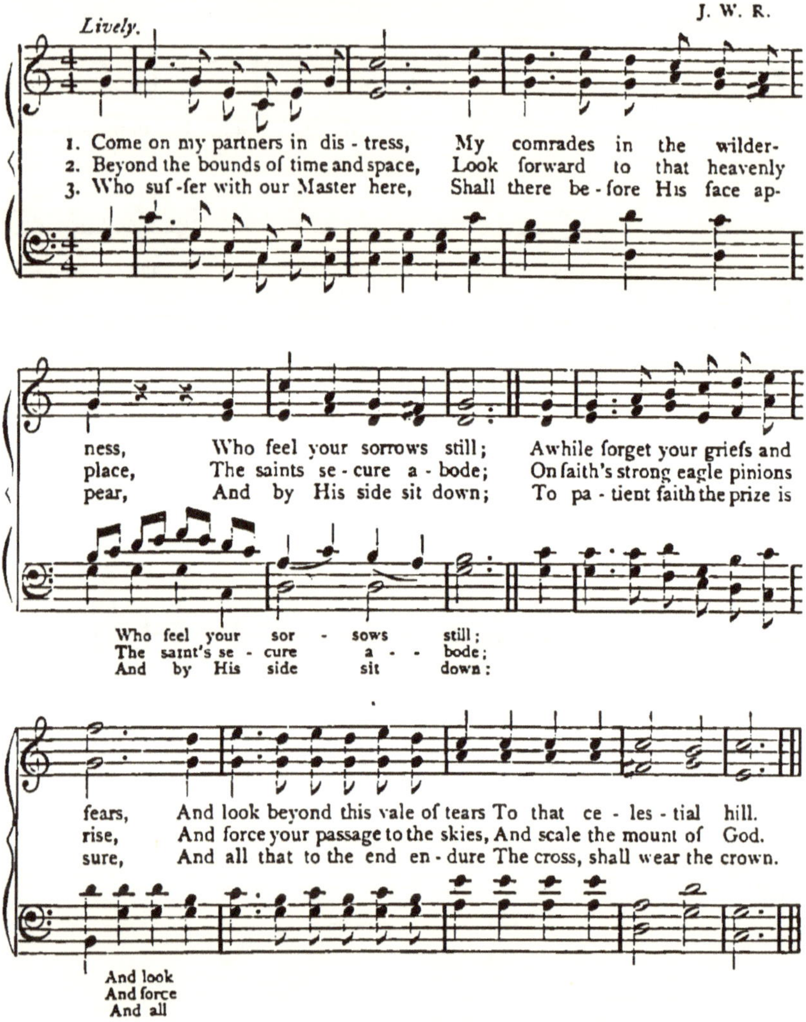
Lively.
1. Come on my partners in dis - tress, My comrades in the wilder-
2. Beyond the bounds of time and space, Look forward to that heavenly
3. Who suf -fer with our Master here, Shall there be - fore His face ap-
ness, Who feel your sorrows still; Awhile forget your griefs and
place, The saints se - cure a - bode; On faith's strong eagle pinions
pear, And by His side sit down; To pa - tient faith the prize is
Who feel your sor - sows still;
The saint's se - cure a - - bode;
And by His side sit down:
fears, And look beyond this vale of tears To that ce - les - tial hill.
rise, And force your passage to the skies, And scale the mount of God.
sure, And all that to the end en - dure The cross, shall wear the crown.
And look
And force
And all

GOD DOTH NOT LEAVE HIS OWN.

J. W. R.

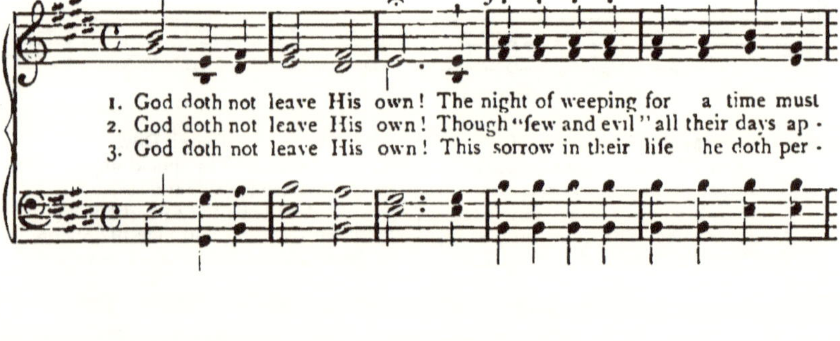
f.
1. God doth not leave His own! The night of weeping for a time must
2. God doth not leave His own! Though "few and evil" all their days ap -
3. God doth not leave His own! This sorrow in their life he doth per -

GOD DOTH NOT LEAVE HIS OWN.
Concluded.

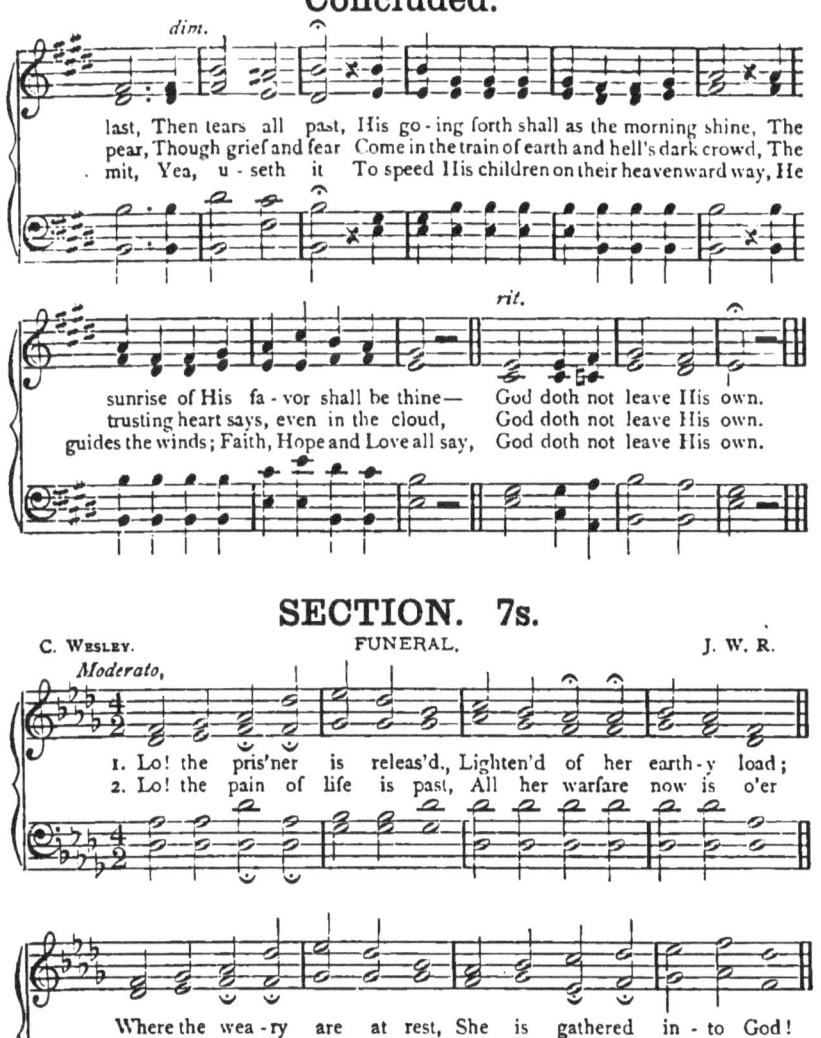

last, Then tears all past, His go-ing forth shall as the morning shine, The
pear, Though grief and fear Come in the train of earth and hell's dark crowd, The
mit, Yea, u-seth it To speed His children on their heavenward way, He

sunrise of His fa-vor shall be thine— God doth not leave His own.
trusting heart says, even in the cloud, God doth not leave His own.
guides the winds; Faith, Hope and Love all say, God doth not leave His own.

SECTION. 7s.

C. WESLEY.   FUNERAL.   J. W. R.

Moderato,

1. Lo! the pris'ner is releas'd., Lighten'd of her earth-y load;
2. Lo! the pain of life is past, All her warfare now is o'er

Where the wea-ry are at rest, She is gathered in-to God!
Death and hell be-hind are cast, Grief and suff'ring are no more.

3. Yes, the Christian's course is run,
   Ended is the glorious strife;
   Fought the fight, the work is done,
   Death is swallow'd up of life!

4. Borne by angels on their wings,
   Far from earth the spirit flies,
   Finds her God, and sits, and sings,
   Triumphing in paradise.

5. Let the world bewail their dead,
   Fondly of their loss complain;
   Sister! friend! by Jesus freed,
   Death, to thee, to us, is gain:

6. Thou art entered into joy:
   Let the unbelievers mourn,
   We in songs our lives employ
   Till we all to God return.

2. Clear as the sun, when from the east,
   Without a cloud he springs,
   And scatters boundless light and heat,
   From his resplendent wings.
   Tremendous as a host that moves
   Majestically slow,
   With banners wide displayed, all armed,
   And fearless of the foe!

PEACE, PEACE ON EARTH.

LAY HIM LOW. Concluded.

3. Farewell to what of earth remains,
Until then,
When exiled spirits shall regain
Forms again!
He died triumphant, bliss to know!
Lay him low, lay him low!

4. Earth to the earth we now resign—
"Rest in peace.'
And dust to dust of kindred kind,
Sweet release,
O cease ye tears, no longer flow,
Lay him low, lay him low!

CANTON. L. M.

J. W. R.

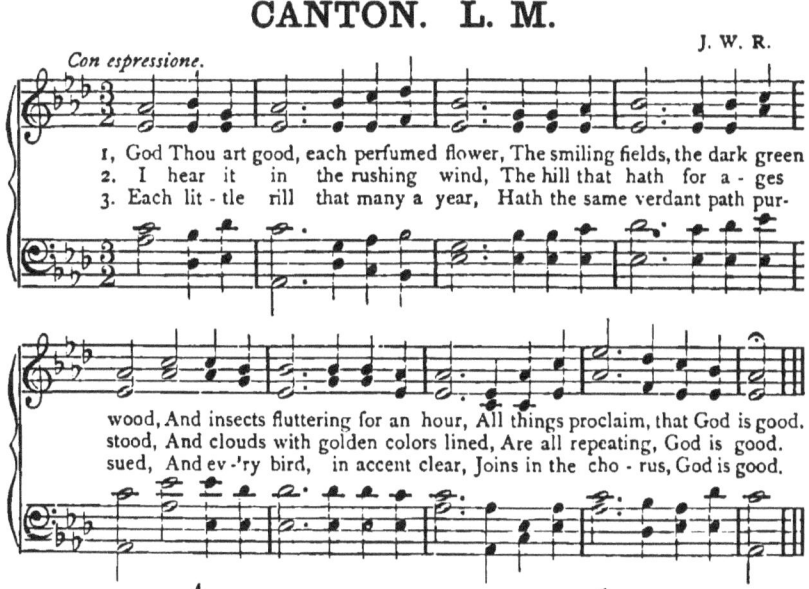

4.
And countless are the blazing stars,
That sing His praise, with light renewed,
The rising sun each day declares,
In rays of glory, God is good.

5.
The moon that walks in brightness, says
That God is good, and we endured
With power to speak our Maker's praise,
Will still repeat that, God is good.

54. ALL BELOW IS BUT A DREAM.

NEWTON.   J. W. R.

1. While with ceaseless course the sun
Hasted through the former year,
Many souls their race have run,
Never more to meet us here,
Never more to meet us here.

2. Fixed in an eternal state,
They have done with all below,
We a little longer wait,
But how little none can know,
But how little none can know.

3. As the wingéd arrow flies
Speedily the mark to find;
As the lightning from the skies
Darts, and leaves no trace behind—

4. Swiftly thus our fleeting days
Bear us down life's rapid stream;
Upward, Lord, our spirits raise,
All below is but a dream.

5. Thanks for mercies past receive,
Pardon for our sins renew;
Teach us henceforth how to live,
With eternity in view;

6. Bless Thy word to old and young,
Fill us with a Saviour's love;
When our life's short race is run,
May we dwell with Thee above.

11s & 10s.

I the Lord will hasten it, etc.

1. DOWN the dark future, through long generations,
The sounds of war grow fainter, and then cease;
And like a bell with solemn, sweet vibrations,
I hear once more the voice of Christ say, "Peace!"

2. Peace! and no longer, from its brazen portals,
The blast of war's great organ shakes the skies;
But beautiful as songs of the immortals,
The holy melodies of love arise.—LONGFELLOW.

FARM-HOUSE. C. M.

J. W. R.

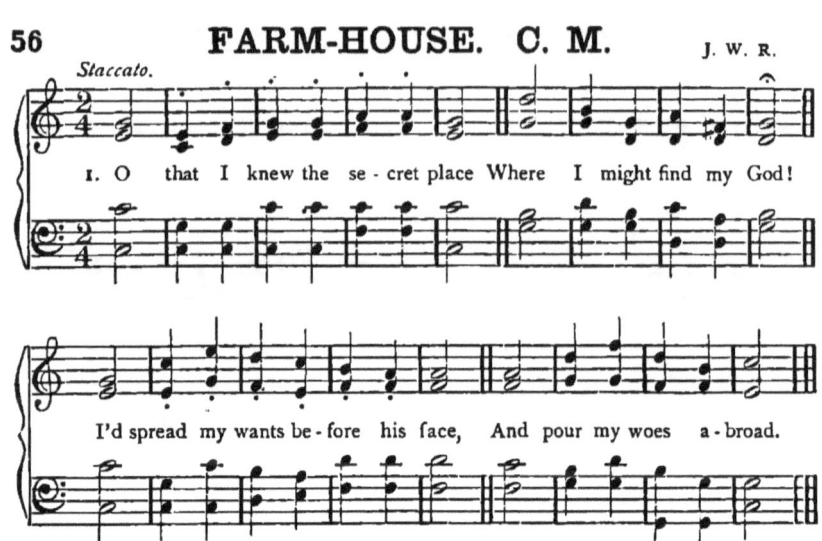

1. O that I knew the secret place Where I might find my God!
I'd spread my wants before his face, And pour my woes abroad.

2.
I'd tell Him how my sins arise;
What sorrows I sustain;
How grace decays, and comfort dies
And leaves my heart in pain.

3.
He knows what arguments I'd take
To wrestle with my God;
I'd plead for His own mercy's sake,
And for my Saviour's blood.

4.
My God, will pity my complaints,
And heal my broken bones;
He takes the meaning of His saints,
The language of their groans.

5.
Arise, my soul from deep distress,
And banish ev'ry fear;
He calls thee to His throne of grace,
To spread thy sorrows there.

MOSSELL.

S. E. SMITH.   MISSIONARY HYMN.   J. W. R.

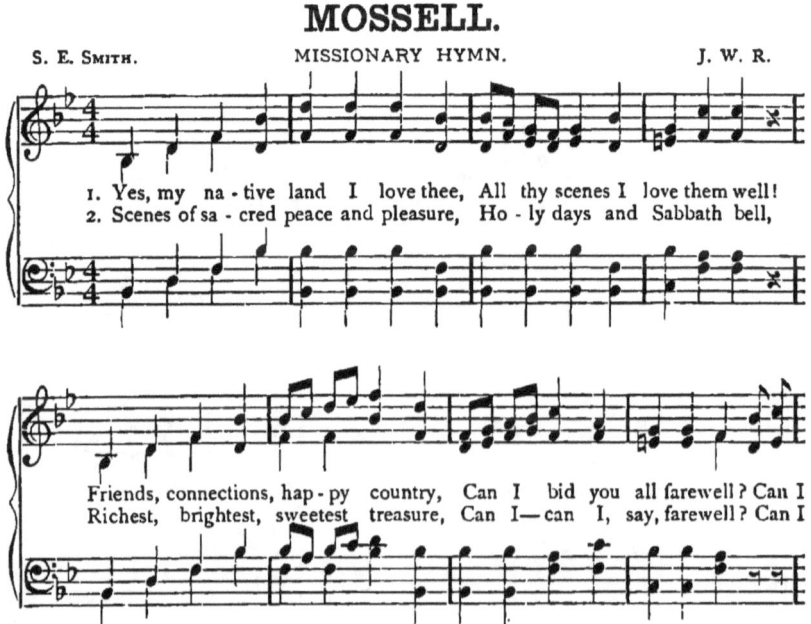

1. Yes, my native land I love thee, All thy scenes I love them well!
2. Scenes of sacred peace and pleasure, Holy days and Sabbath bell,
Friends, connections, happy country, Can I bid you all farewell? Can I
Richest, brightest, sweetest treasure, Can I—can I, say, farewell? Can I

MOSSELL. Concluded.

3. Yes, I hasten from you gladly;
   To the strangers let me tell
   How He died—the blessed Saviour—
   To redeem a world from hell:
   Let me hasten,
   Far in heathen lands to dwell.

4. Bear me on, thou restless ocean,
   From the scenes I love so well:
   Heaves my heart with warm emotion,
   While I go far hence to dwell:
   Glad I bid thee,
   Native land, farewell, farewell!

Hallelujah, Best and Sweetest.

BREVIARY.   J. W. R

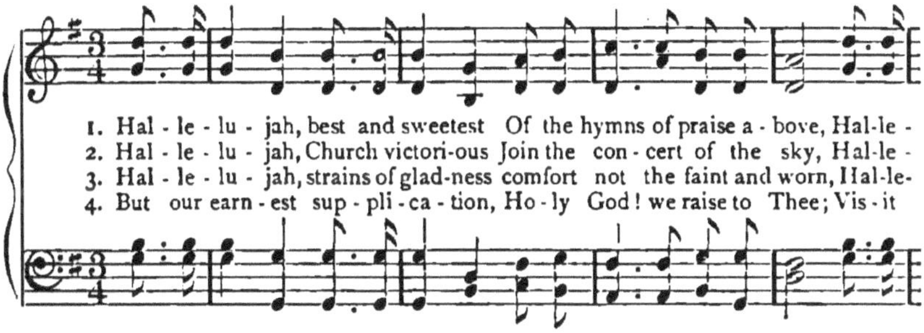

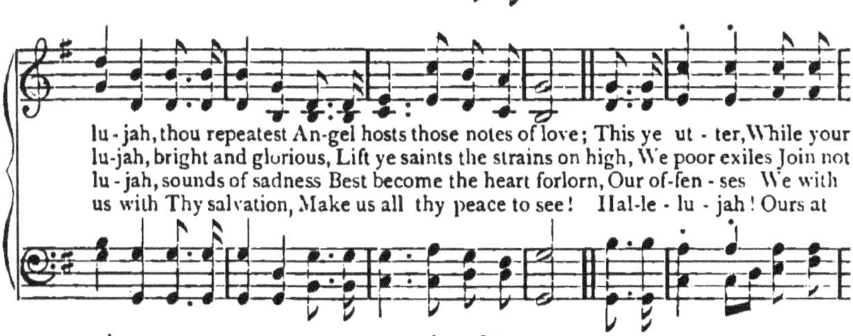

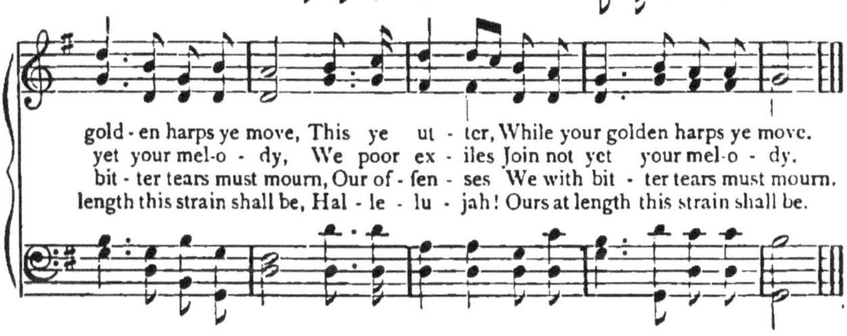

1. Hal-le-lu-jah, best and sweetest Of the hymns of praise a-bove, Hal-le-lu-jah, thou repeatest An-gel hosts those notes of love; This ye ut-ter, While your golden harps ye move, This ye ut-ter, While your golden harps ye move.
2. Hal-le-lu-jah, Church victori-ous Join the con-cert of the sky, Hal-le-lu-jah, bright and glorious, Lift ye saints the strains on high, We poor exiles Join not yet your mel-o-dy, We poor ex-iles Join not yet your mel-o-dy.
3. Hal-le-lu-jah, strains of gladness comfort not the faint and worn, Hal-le-lu-jah, sounds of sadness Best become the heart forlorn, Our of-fen-ses We with bit-ter tears must mourn, Our of-fen-ses We with bit-ter tears must mourn.
4. But our earn-est sup-pli-ca-tion, Ho-ly God! we raise to Thee; Vis-it us with Thy salvation, Make us all thy peace to see! Hal-le-lu-jah! Ours at length this strain shall be, Hal-le-lu-jah! Ours at length this strain shall be.

Jesus, I Love Thy Charming Name.   59

DODDRIDGE.   LEDBETTER.

2.
Yes, thou art precious to my soul,
My transport and my trust;
Jewels, to Thee, are gaudy toys,
And gold is sordid dust.

3.
All my capacious powers can wish
In Thee doth richly meet;
Nor to mine eyes is light so dear,
Nor friendship half so sweet.

ST. JOSEPH. S. M.

Moderato. — J. W. R.

1. Blest be the tie that binds
Our hearts in Christian love;
The fellowship of kindred minds
Is like to that above.

2. Before our Father's throne
We pour our ardent prayers;
Our fears, our hopes our aims, are one,
Our comforts and our cares.

3. We share our mutual woes,
Our mutual burdens bear;
And often for each other flows
The sympathizing tear.

4. Though often called to part,
Amid these scenes of pain;
Yet, we shall still be joined in heart,
And hope to meet again.

5. This glorious hope revives
Our courage by the way;
While each in expectation lives,
And longs to see the day.

6. From sorrow, toil, and pain,
And sin, we shall be free;
And perfect love and friendship reign
Through all eternity.

REEDY'S CHAPPELL. S. M.

WATTS. — J. W. R.

1. Like sheep we went astray, And broke the fold of
2. How dreadful was the hour When God our wanderings
3. How glorious was the grace When Christ sustained the
4. But God hath raised His head O'er all the sons of

REEDY'S CHAPPELL. Concluded. 63

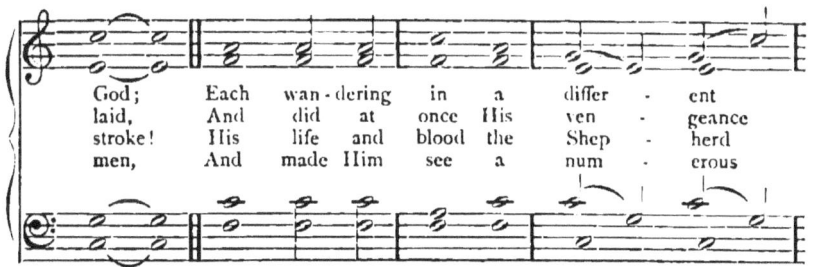

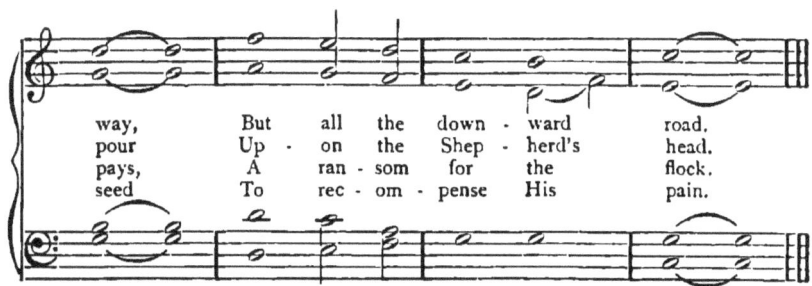

ARMOR. S. M.

BEDDOME.   J. W. R.

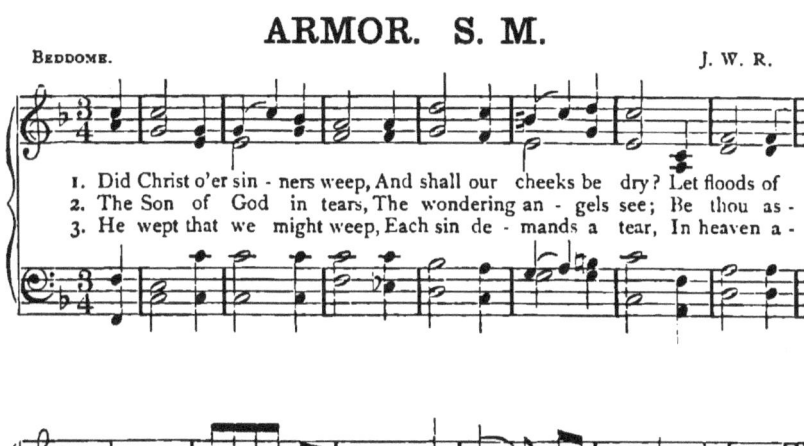

EGYPT. S. M.

NOELS COLL.

1. If on a quiet sea   Towards heaven we calmly sail,
2. But should the surges rise   And rest delay to come,
3. Soon shall our doubts and fears   All yield at Thy control;
4. Teach us, in ev-'ry state,   To make Thy will our own,

With grateful hearts, O God, to Thee,   We'll own the favoring gale, We'll own the favoring gale.
Blest be the sorrow, kind the storm,   Which drives us nearer home, Which drives us nearer home.
Thy tender mercies shall illume   The midnight of the soul, The midnight of the soul.
And, when the joys of sense depart,   To live by faith alone. To live by faith alone.

When Shall I See the Day?

J. MULLEN.

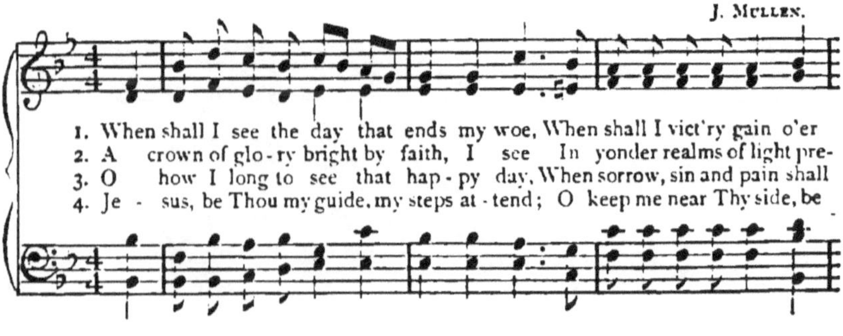

1. When shall I see the day that ends my woe, When shall I vict'ry gain o'er
2. A crown of glory bright by faith, I see In yonder realms of light pre-
3. O how I long to see that happy day, When sorrow, sin and pain shall
4. Jesus, be Thou my guide, my steps attend; O keep me near Thy side, be

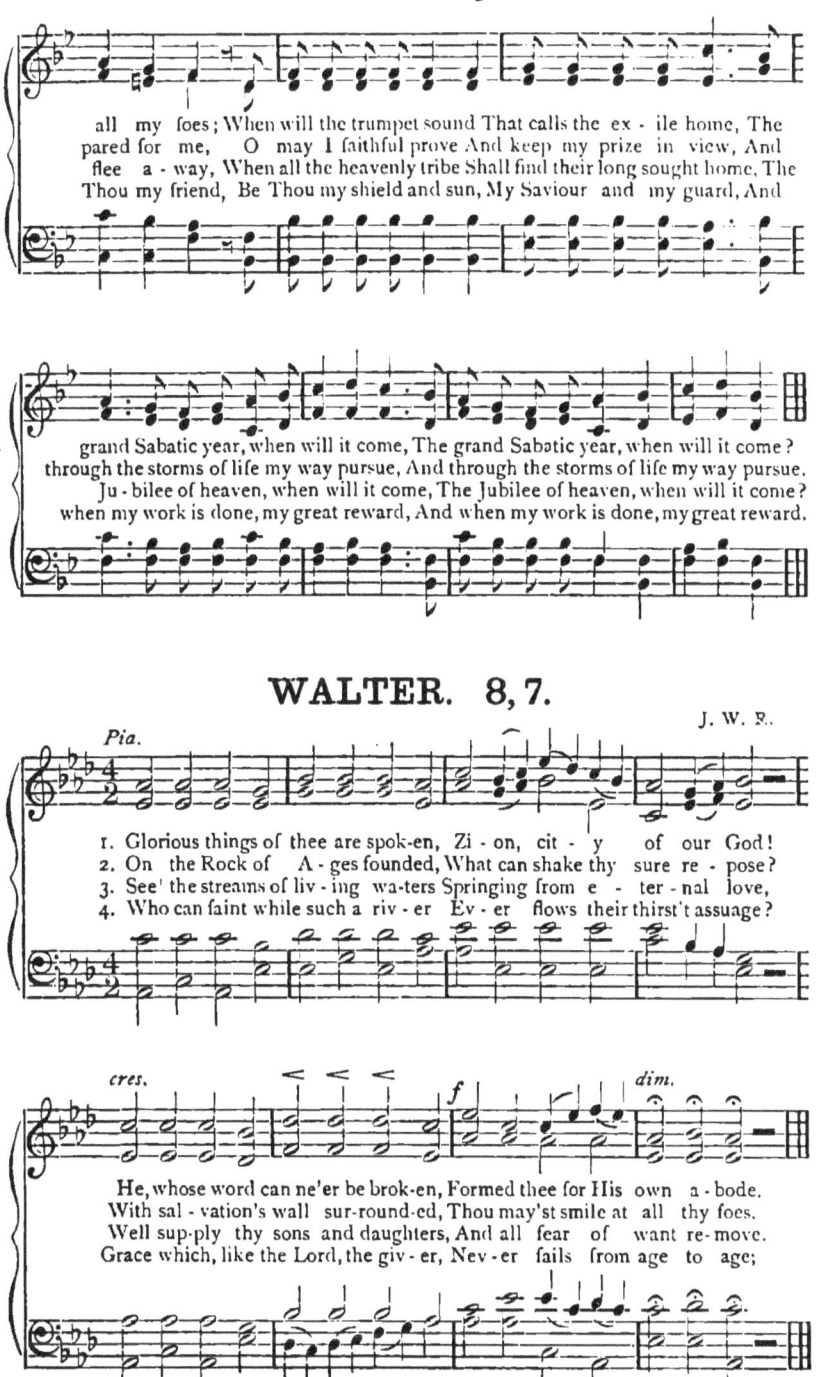

My Rest is in Heaven. Concluded. 67

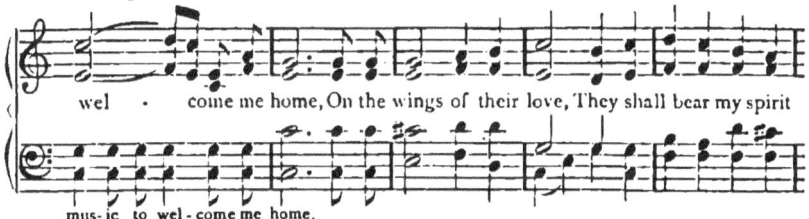

wel - come me home, On the wings of their love, They shall bear my spirit
mus-ic to wel-come me home.

home, A pil-grim and stran-ger no more will I roam.

3. Afflictions may try me, but can not destroy;
One vision of home turns them all into joy;
And the bitterest tear that flows from my eyes,
But sweetens my hope of that home in the skies.

4. Though foes and temptations my progress oppose,
They only make heaven more sweet at the close;
Come joy or come sorrow—the worst may befall,
One moment in heaven will make up for all.

5. The thorn and the thistle around me may grow,
I would not repose upon roses below;
I ask not my portion, I seek not my rest,
'Till seated with Jesus I lean on His breast.

6. A scrip for the way and a staff in my hand,
I march on in haste through the enemy's land:
The road may be rough, but it can not be long;
I'll smooth it with hope, and I'll cheer it with song.

TUNE PEACE, PEACE ON EARTH.   **11s. & 10s.**

That he who loveth God love his brother also.—1. JOHN 4: 21.

1. O HE whom Jesus loved has truly spoken!
   The holier worship which God deigns to bless,
Restores the lost, and heals the spirit broken,
   And feeds the widow and the fatherless.

2. Then, brother man, fold to thy heart thy brother!
   For where loves dwells, the peace of God is there;
To worship rightly is to love each other;
   Each smile a hymn, each kindly deed a prayer.

3. Follow with reverent steps, the great example
   Of Him whose holy work was doing good;
So shall the wide earth seem our Father's temple,
   Each loving life a psalm of gratitude.

4. Thus shall all shackles fall; the stormy clangor
   Of wild war music o'er the earth shall cease;
Love shall tread out the baleful fires of anger,
   And in its ashes plant the tree of peace.—WHITTIER.

68. Hear My Prayer O Lord. Psalm cii.

J. W. R.

Hear My Prayer O Lord. Concluded. 69

me, From me in the day,............... in the day,...............

When I am in trou-ble, in-cline Thine ear un-to me; In the

day when I call, An-swer me speed - i - ly.

HEBRON. C. M.

Timothy Dwight, D, D, 1800,   Dr, L, Mason, 1830,

1. While life prolongs its precious light, Mer - cy is found, and peace is given;
2. While God invites, how blest the day! How sweet the Gospel's charming sound!
3. Soon, borne on time's most rap-id wing, Shall death command you to the grave,

But soon, ah, soon, ap - proaching night Shall blot out ev - 'ry hope of heaven.
Come, sinners, haste, O haste a - way, While yet a pard'ning God is found.
Be - fore his bar your spir - its bring, And none be found to hear or save.

4.
In that lone land of deep despair,
No sabbath's heavenly light shall rise,
No God regard your bitter prayer,
No Saviour call you to the skies.

5.
Now God invites; how blest the day!
How sweet the Gospel's charming sound!
Come, sinners, haste, O haste away,
While yet a pard'ning God is found.

I Wait for Thee. Concluded.

72 THE HARVEST IS PAST.

J. B. Hague.   Jer. 8-20.   J. W. R.

1. Hark, sinner, while God from on high doth entreat thee, And
Give ear to His voice, lest in judgment He meet thee; "The
warnings with accents of mercy do blend;
harvest is passing, the summer will end."

Chorus.

The harvest is passing, The harvest is passing, The harvest is passing, The summer will end.
The harvest is passing the summer will end, The harvest is passing, The summer will end.

2. How oft of thy danger and guilt He hath told thee!
How oft still the message of mercy doth send!
Haste, haste, while He waits in His arms to enfold thee;
"The harvest is passing, the summer will end."

The Harvest is Past. Concluded. 73

3. Despised and rejected, at length He may leave thee;
   What anguish and horror thy bosom will rend!
   Then, haste thee, O sinner, while He will receive thee;
   "The harvest is passing, the summer will end."

4. Ere long, and Jehovah will come in His power;
   Our God will arise, with His foes to contend:
   Haste, haste thee, O sinner; prepare for that hour;
   "The harvest is passing, the summer will end."

5. The Saviour will call thee in judgment before Him:
   O, bow to His sceptre, and make Him thy Friend;
   Now yield Him thy heart; make haste to adore Him;
   "The harvest is passing, the summer will end."

THE LORD'S PRAYER.

Chanting Style.   J. W. R.

Our Father, who art in heaven, Hallowed be Thy Name, Thy kingdom come. Thy will be done on earth, As it is done in heaven. Give us this day our daily bread, Give us this day our daily bread. And forgive us of

MACBETH. 6, 6, 6, 6, 8, 8.

C. Wesley. J. W. R.

1. Ye virgin souls, a-rise, With all the dead a-wake!
   Un-to sal-va-tion wise, Oil in your ves-sels take;

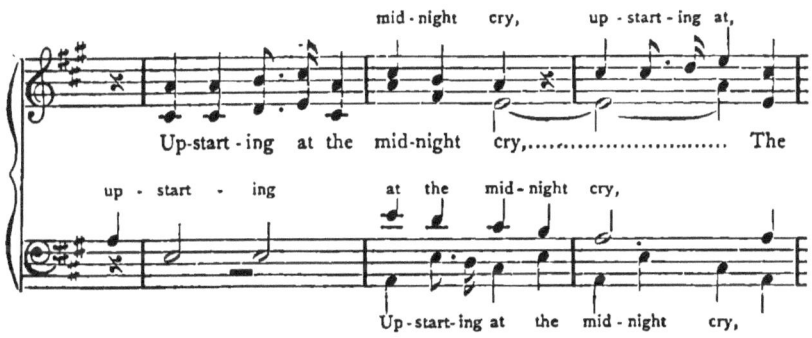

Up-start-ing at the mid-night cry,............ The

midnight cry, "Be-hold............ the heavenly Bride-groom nigh."

2. He comes, He comes, to call
   The nations to His bar,
   And raise to glory all
   Who fit for glory are;
   Made ready for your full reward,
   Go forth with joy to meet your Lord.

3. Go meet Him in the sky,
   Your everlasting Friend;
   Your dead to glorify,
   With all His saints to glorify,
   Ye pure in heart, obtain the grace
   To see, without a veil, His face!

4. The everlasting doors
   Shall soon the saints receive,
   Above you angel powers
   In glorious joy to live;
   Far from a world of grief and sin,
   With God eternally shut in.

COME UNTO ME. Concluded.

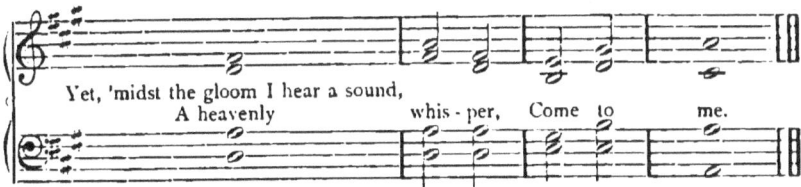

Yet, 'midst the gloom I hear a sound, A heavenly whisper, Come to me.

2.
It tells me of a place of rest—
It tells me where my | soul may | flee;
Oh! to the weary, faint, opprest,
How sweet the | bidding, | Come to | me.

3.
When nature shudders, loth to part
From all I love, en- | joy, and | see,
When a faint chill steals o'er my heart,
A sweet voice | utters, Come to | me.

4.
Come, for all else must fall and die,
Earth is no resting | place for | thee;
Heavenward | direct thy weeping eye,
I am thy | portion, | Come to | me.

5.
O voice of mercy! voice of love!
In conflict, grief, and—ago- | ny,
Support me, cheer me from above!
And gently | whisper, | Come to | me.

"JUST AS I AM." Chant. No. 2.

Him that cometh unto me, I will in no wise cast out.—JOHN vi : 37

1. Just as I am without one plea, But that Thy blood was shed for me, And that Thou bidd'st me come to Thee, O Lamb of God, I come.

2. Just as I am, and waiting not To rid my soul of one dark blot— To Thee whose blood can cleanse each spot, O Lamb of God, I come.

3.
Just as I | am, though tossed a- | bout |
With many a | conflict, many a | doubt, |
With fears within, and foes without—
O Lamb of | God, I | come.

4.
Just as I | am, poor, wretched, | blind; |
Sight, riches, | healing of the | mind, |
Yea, all I need, in Thee to find,
O Lamb of | God, I | come.

5.
Just as I | am, Thou wilt re- | ceive, |
Wilt welcome, | pardon, cleanse, re | lieve,
Because Thy promise I believe—
O Lamb of | God, I | come.

6.
Just as I | am—Thy love un- | known, |
Has broken | every barrier | down; |
Now to be Thine, yea, Thine alone,
O Lamb of | God, I | come.

GENTILITY. L. M.

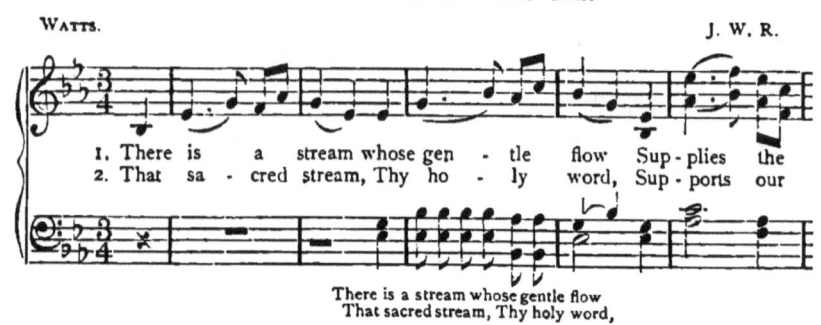

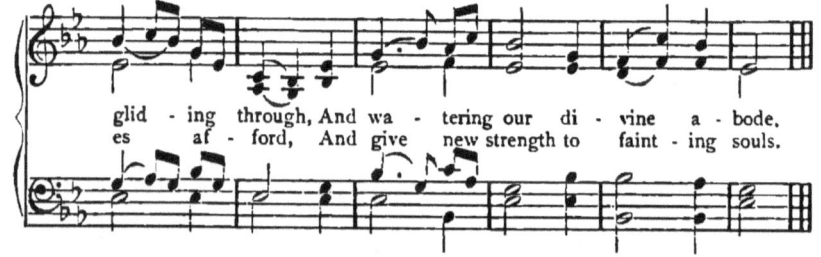

MT. TABOR. L. M.

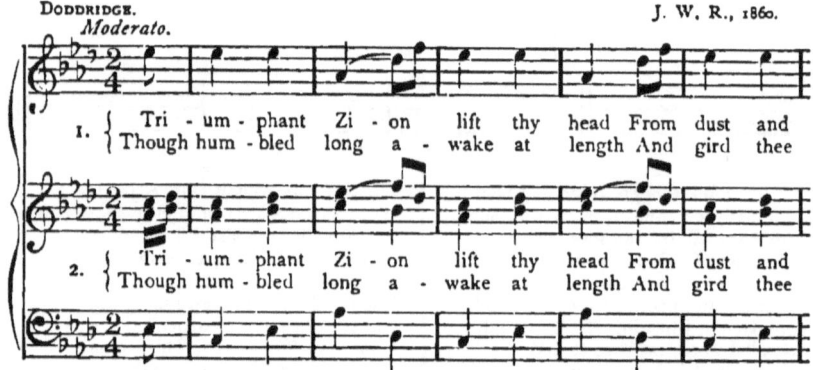

MT. TABOR. Concluded.

3.
No more shall foes unclean invade,
And fill thy hallowed walls with dread;
No more shall hell's insulting host
Their victory and thy sorrows boast.

4.
God, from on high, has heard thy prayer;
His hand thy ruins shall repair:
Nor will thy watchful Monarch cease
To guard thee in eternal peace.

WAITING AND FIGHTING.

J. W. R.

1. Christians are you waiting for the Saviour, Christians are you waiting for the Saviour, Christians are you waiting for the Saviour? Calling you in love.
Saying to His servants, well and faithful, Saying to His servants well and faithful, Saying to His servants, well and faithful, To your home above.

2. Soldiers are you fighting for the Saviour, Soldiers are you fighting for the Saviour, Soldiers are you fighting for the Saviour? Soon the war will close.
And upon the fields of endless glory, And upon the fields of endless glory, And upon the fields of endless glory, You shall have repose.

Chorus.
If in Jesus we believe, Crowns of glory we'll receive, In the mansions of the faithful; If in Jesus we believe, Crowns of glory we'll receive, In the mansions of the blest.

82 WARD. L. M.

WATTS. J. W. R.

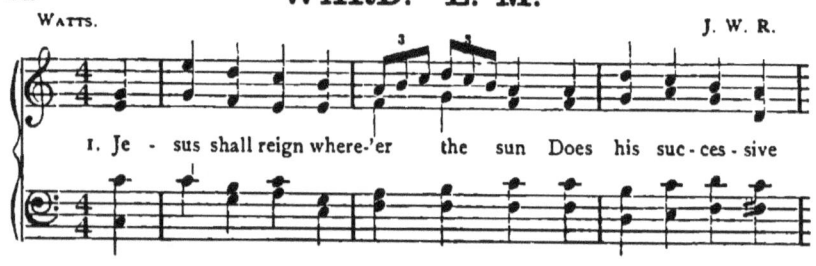
1. Je-sus shall reign where-'er the sun Does his suc-ces-sive

jour-neys run; His kingdom stretch from shore to shore, Till moons shall

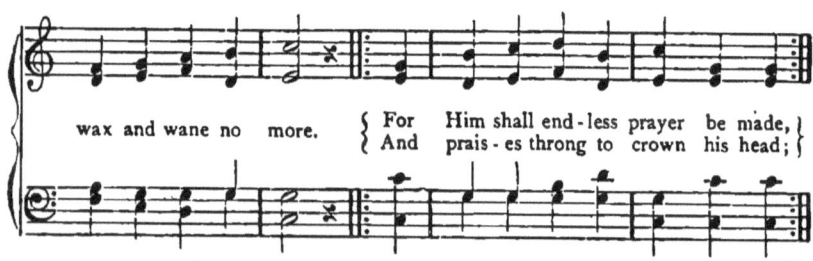
wax and wane no more. { For Him shall end-less prayer be made, } { And prais-es throng to crown his head; }

His name like sweet per-fume shall rise With ev'ry morn-ing sac-ri-fice.

2.
People and realms of every tongue
Dwell on His love with sweetest song;
And infant voices shall proclaim
Their early blessings on His name.
Blessings abound where'er he reigns;
The prisoner leaps to loose His chains,
The weary find eternal rest,
And all the sons of want are blest.

3.
Where He displays His healing power.
Death and the curse are known no more;
In Him the tribes of Adam boast
More blessings than their father lost.
Let every creature rise, and bring
Peculiar honors to our King;
Angels descend with songs again,
And earth repeat the long Amen.

INDEX TO PIECES.

A
	PAGE.
Absence. S. M	24
A Crown of life	5
Advocate. 8s, 7s, 4s	37
Ah, guilty sinner	27
All below is but a dream	54
All is well	42
And let our bodies. S. M	20
Aragon. C. M	50
As down in the sunless	21
As far as the East	58
Armor. S. M	63
Ava	47
Away to the water of life	28

B
Balmorel. S. M	29
Behold Thy King, O Zion	40

C
Canton. L. M	53
Castington. L. M	32
Champ. C. P. M	48
City of Gold	4
Cleanse me now	40
Come unto me. Chant	76
Come to the overflowing	19
Come ye thankful people. 7s double	22
Come Lord Jesus	26
Come and unite	30
Consolation. 6, 4	76
Coronation. C. M	31
Cyrus. S. M	33

D
Delay not	36
Dover. S. M	12
Down the dark future. 11s, & 10s	54

E
Easter hymn	14
Egypt. S. M	64
Exaltation. L. M	18

F
Far down the ages now. S. M	24
Farm house. C. M	56
Fountain. C. M	31
Fraternity	11
Freedom's Jubilee	16

G
Gentility. L. M	78
God doth not leave His own!	48

H
Hallelujah, best and sweetest	57
Hasten, O hasten!	8
Hear my prayer	68
Heaven	61
Hebron. C. M	69
Hodly. L. M	9

I
It is well	60
I wait for thee	70

J
Jesus, I love Thy	59

	PAGE.
Just as I am. Chant	77

L
Lay him low. Funeral	52
Lula. 7s	23

M
Macbeth. 6, 6, 6, 6, 8, 8	75
Manteo. L. M	28
March forth to the conflict	13
Mark the soft falling snow	42
Mid scenes of confusion. 11s	35
Missionary hymn. 7s, & 6s	46
Mossell. Missionary Hymn	56
Mt. Tabor. L. M	78
Must Simon bear the Cross alone	35
My God I am Thine	44
My rest is in heaven	66

N
No night in heaven	43
No sickness there	7

O
O He whom Jesus loved. 11s, & 10s	67
Old Hundred. L. M	20

P
Peace, Peace on earth	51
Palms of Glory	18
Plymouth. 6, 6, 6, 8, 8	25
Park street. L. M	22
Parting hymn	12

R
Reedy's Chappell. S. M	62

S
Saved by faith	9
Seasons. C. M	36
Section. 7s	49
Sinner go, will you go?	32
Star of Redemption	55
St. Joseph. S. M	62

T
The home of the soul	45
The house of prayer	3
The harvest is past	72
The Lord's Prayer	73
The mercy seat. L. M	81
The Nativity	38
The night song	10
Tribute. L. M	15
Tiviola. L. M	52

W
Waiting and fighting	80
Walter. 8, 7	65
Ward. L. M	82
When silent night	34
When shall I see the day	64
When the Lord shall appear	6
Why will ye waste. L. M	17
Windham. Old tune. L. M	17
Wilberforce. S. M	39
With sacred joy. C. M	20
Wright. C. M	24

www.ingramcontent.com/pod-product-compliance
Lightning Source LLC
Chambersburg PA
CBHW020324090426
42735CB00009B/1393